D1273280

‘FOUR QUARTETS’ REHEARSED

'FOUR QUARTETS' REHEARSED

A Commentary on
T. S. Eliot's Cycle of Poems

By

RAYMOND PRESTON

LONDON
SHEED & WARD
1948

FIRST PUBLISHED 1946
BY SHEED AND WARD, LTD.
110/111 FLEET STREET,
LONDON, E.C.4
FOURTH IMPRESSION 1948

ACKNOWLEDGEMENT

My thanks are due to the author and to Messrs. Faber & Faber for permission to reproduce the many quotations from the works of T. S. Eliot which are included in this volume.

PRINTED IN GREAT BRITAIN
BY PURNELL AND SONS, LTD.
PAULTON (SOMERSET) AND LONDON

PREFACE

MR. ELIOT once said—I do not know how seriously—that he would prefer an illiterate audience; and an illiterate audience might at least possess the honesty and humility which are sometimes lacking among his literate critics. Poetry can be enjoyed but not criticized before it is understood; and a pretence of understanding will not serve as a basis of criticism—or of anything else except a deplorable form of snobbery. By understanding *Four Quartets* I mean more, of course, than the ability to produce a paraphrase of a given passage that will pass muster: I mean a *possession* of the poems which may, together with the ability to see them in relation to the European tradition of religious verse, take the place of criticism. The aim of this book is mainly to deal with obstacles in the way of understanding which readers of *Four Quartets* may encounter. I have tried not to avoid any of the difficulties which I have myself found; and I am indebted to those with whom I have discussed the poems for suggesting others and for their help in meeting them. I am aware that 'explanation' of poetry can very easily falsify it. But a commentary which contains honest attempts at explanation is in a modest if only negative way more useful than a commentary which is a series of evasions. I have in mind two reasons for making these attempts: they may provide a few signposts for many readers of the poems; and they will for all readers bring out by contrast the mastery of the original language. And the second point is as important as the first. For here—I assume that the reader has the poems by him—is a voice which compels attention and commands understanding, a medium which is hard and which cuts clean, a language which is charged with controlled suggestion. And it is this compelling quality which leads us to feel as we read many passages those 'moments of happiness', that 'sudden illumination' which Mr. Eliot has done more than speak of; to feel that though

> We had the experience but missed the meaning,
> And approach to the meaning restores the experience
> In a different form . . .

the power of the poetry is such that we cannot rest until we have both 'experience' and 'meaning'. And it is the *arriving* at the meaning, not the explaining of it, that matters. Anyone who attempts to 'elucidate' *Four Quartets* must be aware all the time that the poems themselves supply the light.

I wish to thank Mr. Eliot for reading the first draft of this essay and for adding some interesting notes. It would be ungracious not to express my gratitude for his kindly encouragement, but presumptuous to suggest that this is in any sense an 'authorized' commentary. It is an attempt to indicate what the poetry means for one reader. Whether it is more than that is for other readers to decide.

NOTE

THE title *Four Quartets* covers the four poems *Burnt Norton*, *East Coker*, *The Dry Salvages*, and *Little Gidding*, which are discussed in that order in the following pages. It has been pointed out that the technique of Eliot's poetry resembles the thematic statement and development of music, and the title is appropriate for related reasons, two of which I suggest on page 41 and page 51 of the present essay. Another point to which the title draws our attention has been stated by Herbert Read in a comment on some of his own poems:

> 'They constitute a search for a form for the long poem which is not merely a continuation of the same thing more or less indefinitely (blank verse, rhymed couplets, etc.), or an addition of identical units (a sonnet sequence), but a poem on the analogy of *the Quartet in music*, with separate movements, forms within the form, diversity within unity. . . .'[1]

It needs to be added that Eliot's poems constitute a search for something more than a poetic form: the poetic form has been found. Miss Helen Gardner has already described the form in an essay, to which I shall refer again, called 'The Recent Poetry of T. S. Eliot' and published by the Hogarth Press in *New Writing and Daylight*, Summer, 1942.

The two Greek epigraphs to *Burnt Norton* are taken from the *Fragments* of the early Greek philosopher Heraclitus. I quote two versions of the first:

> 'Therefore it is a duty to follow the common law. But although the Logos ("Word") is common to all, the majority of people live as though they had an understanding of their own' (Diels: *Encyclopædia of Religion and Ethics*). 'The law of things is a law of Reason Universal, but most men live as though they had a wisdom of their own' (J. M. Mitchell).

[1] Quoted from *Herbert Read, an Introduction to his Work*, edited by Henry Treece. (Faber & Faber, 1944).

It should be pointed out that these are particular interpretations, and that others are possible: Mr. Eliot says that he was attracted by the *poetic suggestiveness* of the fragments.

I give John Burnet's translation of the second epigraph:

'The way up and the way down is one and the same.'

The epigraph is used by Mr. Eliot in *The Dry Salvages:*

> And the way up is the way down, the way forward is the way back.

'FOUR QUARTETS' REHEARSED

I

ALTHOUGH parts of *Burnt Norton* make an immediate and unforgettable impression at a first reading, the whole poem is in my experience more difficult than any of the three which follow. Those who first read it in the edition of collected poems published in 1936 certainly had been given a start; but I am inclined to think that the reader who sees it for the first time as one of the *Four Quartets* has the advantage. He will find that there are some things at the beginning of the journey which are suddenly lit up as he proceeds.

We may imagine that the poem had its origin in one of those 'rare moments of inattention and detachment' to which Mr. Eliot refers in an essay[1] that was probably written about the same time; and we may imagine the experience taking place in the garden of a Gloucestershire country house called Burnt Norton[2]—a garden which seems to have suggested much of the imagery of the poem. But the illuminating vision is not easily come by, and the poet refuses to pretend that it is: hence the perplexity of the opening lines. And because in these lines he appears to be hazarding dialectic one tends to assume that his poem will be, in the literal sense, logical. Logical thought will help us to understand the poem, but it cannot be appreciated by logical thought alone. *Burnt Norton* attempts a less mediate apprehension of reality than discursive reasoning can by itself achieve.

The first few lines might be taken as a meditation on the words of *Ecclesiastes*:

> 'That which hath been is now; and that which is to be hath already been; and God requireth that which is past' (iii. 15).

Eliot is turning over an idea which is stated in the simplest possible terms later in the poem: '. . . and all is always now.'

[1] The essay on John Marston, in *Selected Essays* (Faber & Faber, 1934), p. 232.
[2] This was only a point of departure for the poem. Mr. Eliot says that he was unacquainted with the history of the place.

It is an idea which is later to be worked out poetically in terms of individual experience, racial experience, and the pattern of history; and we do not understand what the poet is here groping towards until we see his beginning in relation to the lines

> . . . Not the intense moment
> Isolated, with no before and after,
> But a lifetime burning in every moment
> And not the lifetime of one man only
> But of old stones that cannot be deciphered.
>
> *East Coker*

and

> Men's curiosity searches past and future
> And clings to that dimension. But to apprehend
> The point of intersection of the timeless
> With time, is an occupation for the saint—
>
> *The Dry Salvages*

and

> . . . This is the use of memory:
> For liberation—not less of love but expanding
> Of love beyond desire, and so liberation
> From the future as well as the past.
>
> *Little Gidding*

But this confidence has to be fought for. *Burnt Norton* opens with 'echoes' which are difficult to catch: the *perhaps* is not there by accident. But the following lines spoken by Harry in *The Family Reunion* will help us to follow the speculation:

> . . . all past is present, all degradation
> Is unredeemable. As for what happens—
> Of the past you can only see what is past,
> Not what is always present. That is what matters.

'Your ordinary murderer', he says,

> cannot realize
> That everything is irrevocable,
> The past unredeemable.[1]

[1] *The Family Reunion* (Faber & Faber, 1939), pp. 29 and 67.

But Harry is not Mr. Eliot: there is no note of hysteria in the lines of *Burnt Norton*:

> If all time is eternally present
> All time is unredeemable.

And the verse of this poem is more controlled: it implies a determination to endure intellectual uncertainty (Keats's 'negative capability') and at the same time to register faithfully the fluctuations of feeling that accompany it:

> What might have been is an abstraction
> Remaining a perpetual possibility
> Only in a world of speculation.

'To the abstracting mind of man', we might paraphrase, 'an unrealized potential event does not cease to be potential.' Alter the syntax and remove the line divisions, and the effect has gone. In the verse the qualification of the last line is retarded; the reader, having been buoyed up by the second line, is lowered to sea-level. Place the word *only* at the end instead of at the beginning of the line, and the reader is dropped. The *perpetual possibility* is not illusion, and the emphasis is on the *world of speculation*. The short yet deliberate sentences suggest a series of carefully aimed shots at a point which is only just visible; and what follows is a bold shot which we are almost convinced has reached the mark, but what the mark is we are not yet certain:

> What might have been and what has been
> Point to one end, which is always present.

If the *one end* is the divine purpose, it is not very surprising that we are uncertain about it; we only know that these two bearings—*what might have been* and *what has been*—indicate a goal outside time. The lines insist on 'what might have been', on what we deeply desire to be, on what in some sense—they hint—*is*, though not in time, and not in appearance. (Compare Harry's line: 'And what did not happen is as true as what did happen.'[1]) The poet is expressing a state which is neither faith nor doubt: he is *on the edge* of faith.

[1] *The Family Reunion*, p. 108.

But these lines dissolve appearance, if they do not yet reveal the reality. Agatha's words in *The Family Reunion* express more diffusely but in similar terms the experience which is in the lines of *Burnt Norton* universalized:

> I only looked through the little door
> When the sun was shining on the rose-garden:
> And heard in the distance tiny voices
> And then a black raven flew over.
> And then I was only my own feet walking
> Away, down a concrete corridor
> In a dead air. Only feet walking
> And sharp heels scraping. Over and under
> Echo and noise of feet. . . .
>
> *The Family Reunion* (p. 107)

> Footfalls echo in the memory
> Down the passage which we did not take
> Towards the door we never opened
> Into the rose-garden. . . .
>
> *Burnt Norton*

Like the *logos* of Heraclitus[1] this memory exists in common, although we rarely become aware of it.

Then there is the sudden vision; and it has the vividness and intimacy of a personal experience. But although it is so close, so compelling—suggesting, as Eliot can suggest so intensely, pristine sensuous impressions such as are half-remembered from childhood—it is explicitly not oppressive: only 'echoes' inhabit the garden, and instead of swooning with the scent of the roses, they are

> Moving without pressure, over the dead leaves, . . .

The *rose-garden* is the Garden 'where all loves end' of *Ash-Wednesday*, and the 'last of earth left to discover' of *Little Gidding*. It is 'our first world', 'that which was the beginning', the Earthly Paradise. The rose carries the sexual and religious associations of the *Roman de la Rose* and the mystic rose of the *Paradiso*.

[1] See the first epigraph to the poem.

> But to what purpose
> Disturbing the dust on a bowl of rose-leaves
> I do not know.

The juxtaposition of the dead rose-leaves and the living rose-garden effected by these lines which introduce the vision is characteristic: a way of urging the reader to see and to feel and at the same time maintaining a detachment from nostalgic indulgence. It conveys the doubt and hesitation of the opening in imagery.

The allegory of the rose-garden is presented as poignantly as that scene in *The Waste Land:*

> —Yet when we came back, late, from the Hyacinth garden, . . .

Here, too, is the *heart of light:*[1]

> And the pool was filled with water out of sunlight,
> And the lotos rose, quietly, quietly,
> The surface glittered out of heart of light, . . .
> Then a cloud passed, and the pool was empty.

This is the joy of Eden, shattered when the divine light is withdrawn.

> Go, go, go, said the bird: human kind
> Cannot bear very much reality.

The symbolism used by Eliot recurs and gathers richness as it does so. We have only to remember the hermit-thrush of *The Waste Land* to understand the phrase *the deception of the thrush:* to begin with, the poet half feels that it is only leading him up the garden path. The phrase also refers to the elusive darting of the bird, previously suggested in the verse. And the bird of this poem reminds us of the one suggested in *Ash-Wednesday* in allusion to Grimm's tale, *The*

[1] Reminiscent of Dante's *del cor dell' una delle luci nuove* . . . (*Paradiso,* XII. 28). And the beautiful effect of repetition in the second line of the quotation may be compared with

> *sì soprastando al lume intorno intorno* . . .

which should be read in its context (*Paradiso,* XXX. 112).

Juniper-Tree, and of that in *Ecclesiastes*, Chapter xii.[1] It is both an expected presence in the garden, and a miraculous messenger.

The section closes with a reminder of its opening, now more fully understood. Time perceived in growth, movement and change presupposes a stillness, completeness and permanence—the fullness of reality which human kind cannot bear. As well as what has happened, 'what might have been' has a meaning and a constant value—a perfection we can imagine, hinting at the 'one end' which as we pursue our limited or never realized aims we do not see. We might say that the 'one end' includes and transcends the apparent flux of time, but Mr. Eliot is not philosophizing. He is striving towards the 'disciplined dream' of Dante as the means of a fuller consciousness:

> Time past and time future
> Allow but a little consciousness.
> To be conscious is not to be in time
> But only in time can the moment in the rose-garden . . .
> Be remembered; involved with past and future.
> Only through time time is conquered.

The vision of Section I includes evidence of time, change, decay: the dust on the bowl of rose-leaves, the dead leaves, the autumn heat. But it is the triumph of the poetry that it nevertheless succeeds in suggesting an experience which is timeless. The climax of the allegory depends on the fact that in the pool in which the lotos rises and the roses are reflected *there is no water :* appearance is forgotten in the vision of reality. In *The Hollow Men*,

> Between the potency
> And the existence . . .
> Falls the Shadow.

Here no Shadow falls while the vision lasts. Events and succession of events, what happened and what did not happen, cease to matter. What matters is *fullness of being*.

[1] Grimm's bird is also a miraculous agent. The phrase from *Ecclesiastes* which I have in mind is: ' . . . he shall rise up at the voice of the bird' (xii. 4).

As my last quotation from the poem indicates, the first movement is made clearer by Section II; and in this connexion I wish to draw attention to a key-phrase of the second strophe of that section: 'Neither flesh nor fleshless.' The imagery of the rose-garden appears in *The Family Reunion* at the rare moments when there *is* reunion—a genuine understanding, a real relationship between Harry and Mary or between Harry and Agatha. The suggestion of *human relations* in the mention of 'children' and of 'guests' is not the whole meaning of the vision of the rose-garden in *Burnt Norton*, but is that part of it which makes the communication of the whole meaning possible.

The first strophe of Section II forms the most diverse images into a pattern: one's first impression is that here more than anywhere else in the poem is a symbolist construction rather than a statement. First the feeling is earth-bound, then as free as the leaves dancing in light; and we seem to see the purified essence of what we have known, with the accidents of our life removed and its conflicts resolved. The effect is described in the third strophe:

> . . . both a new world
> And the old made explicit, understood
> In the completion of its partial ecstasy,
> The resolution of its partial horror.

The thread of life and consciousness, 'the trilling wire in the blood',

> Sings below inveterate scars
> And reconciles forgotten wars.
> The dance along the artery
> The circulation of the lymph
> Are figured in the drift of stars . . .

It is a vision of the ordered universe in which movement from one part of it to another seems so effortless that it is not movement at all, and it is the whole of which we are conscious, not the part. The strophe begins with a strangely potent, concentrated sense-impression:

> Garlic and sapphires in the mud
> Clot the bedded axle-tree. . . .

This, according to Mr. Eliot, was suggested by a line of Mallarmé's sonnet, *M'introduire dans ton histoire . . .:*

Tonnerre et rubis aux moyeux

which in a similar way hits two senses at once (Mallarmé deafens and dazzles us in a single line). It is possible to provide notes on the literary associations of sapphires and axle-trees, but I am inclined to think that more important than any meaning we may subsequently find for the images, is the nature of their immediate impact. Strong sense-impressions which are normally experienced *in succession* are in these two lines registered *simultaneously;* and they suggest a third sensation —arrested movement. I take this as a way of imagining existence outside time—a way of suggesting what is meant by 'time is conquered'. Another way is attempted in the second strophe, and it seems to me that the point of the first strophe is largely to throw the second into relief.[1] We should note, however, the relation between *the bedded axle-tree* and *the still point of the turning world:* the 'axle-tree' can mean the axis upon which the world turns.

I can best bring out what I think is the point of the remainder of this section and the ideas behind certain other parts of the *Four Quartets* by quoting the following from St. Thomas Aquinas:

> '. . . By means of the ordering of all things, which has been as it were projected out of Him and which bears certain images and likenesses of its divine patterning, we ascend in ordered degrees so far as we are able to that which is above all things, by the ways of negation and transcendence, and the conception of a universal cause.
>
> 'Thus God is known in all things and yet apart from all things; and He is known through knowledge and through ignorance. On the one hand, He is apprehended by intuition, reason, understanding, touch, sense, opinion, imagination, name, and so on; while on the other hand He cannot be grasped by intuition nor can He be uttered or named, and He is not anything in the world, nor is He known in any existent thing' (*The Book of the Blessed Dionysius concerning the Divine Names:* vii, lect. 4).

[1] I feel that the contrast is similar to that in *East Coker*, Section II, though not so strong.

The first strophe leads up, in the Dantesque manner, to the stars. It is a poetic form suggesting the *Erhebung*[1] of the third strophe. Now the poet, holding on to his positive image:

> At the still point of the turning world . . .[2]

proceeds by the only way which can take him further—the 'way of negation'. It is as if he cannot say more of what eternity is like, except by saying what it is *not* like, by successively rejecting ideas which limit the 'one end'; and the process is as fascinating as an operation performed with aplomb and precision by a blind surgeon.

What I have just said may perhaps be misleading in two ways. For one thing it may appear that I have limited St. Thomas's words to the problem of expression: that was not intended. Secondly, Mr. Eliot does not even mention the word 'eternity', and it can hardly be said that he is defining it: that is the job of the philosopher or theologian. He is rather trying to *divine* the condition itself, to realize as precisely as possible what 'eternal life' is from the hints given by—not thought alone, but perception and feeling and thought. It is as much an activity of the sensibility as of the intelligence, for it requires no mere concentration of the intellect, but a focusing of the whole personality. The poet had the vision, the experience, and approach to its meaning restores it *in a different form*, a form greater than the experience as it appeared in time:[3]

> I can only say, *there* we have been: but I cannot say where.
> And I cannot say, how long, for that is to place it in time.

I have mentioned two kinds of statement in these poems: there is a third, which is the nearest to what we call 'plain speech'. If you are trying to say anything which is at all difficult to express, plain speech is inaccurate—imprecise as

[1] 'Elevation' is the nearest English equivalent—avoided, I suppose, for reasons of euphony.

[2] The motif of this section first occurs in *Triumphal March:*

> O hidden under the dove's wing, hidden in the turtle's breast
> Under the palm-tree at noon, under the running water
> At the still point of the turning world. O hidden.

[3] Here I am referring to lines in *The Dry Salvages*, Section II.

an expression of thought, crude as an expression of feeling. It requires qualification, which frequently in Eliot takes the concentrated form of paradox; it may be further concentrated and enriched by such means as ellipsis, anaphora,[1] and even play on words; and its tempo, pause and stress can be made to convey nuances of meaning through a controlled interaction of syntax, line-division and punctuation. As Eliot himself has reminded us in the ninth chorus from *The Rock* and in these poems, words decay and crumble with daily misuse; and it is one function of the poet to revive them, 'to purify the dialect of the tribe'. The common word may be forced in the hands of a master of language to take on a new solidity, a new sharpness of outline, and even a meaning which is different from the accepted one:

Time past and time future
Allow but a little consciousness.
To be conscious is not to be in time . . .

If this is a matter of technique, we should remember that technique is not the fruit of a mere dabbling in word patterns. It may even be said to be, in this poetry, a moral matter; for it means making currency equivalent to goods—although, absolutely, it is only the goods that matter ('the poetry does not matter'). The use of words in an intellectual game of conceptual counters (to borrow a phrase of Maritain's) could not produce a charge of meaning like this:

. . . the enchainment of past and future
Woven in the weakness of the changing body,
Protects mankind from heaven and damnation
Which flesh cannot endure.

In struggling towards a discipline of spirit through a discipline of language, Eliot has re-affirmed in his own practice the value of poetry.

The first part of Section III deals with the everyday world, in which there is the reverse of

[1] *i.e.* the repetition of the same word or phrase in successive clauses.

> The inner freedom from the practical desire,
> The release from action and suffering, release from the inner
> And the outer compulsion, . . .

There is in it an apparent return to an earlier note in Mr. Eliot's work—a note of disgust, first intensified then sublimated:

> Men and bits of paper, whirled by the cold wind
> That blows before and after time,
> Wind in and out of unwholesome lungs
> Time before and time after.
> Eructation of unhealthy souls
> Into the faded air, the torpid
> Driven on the wind that sweeps the gloomy hills of London . . .

This is not merely a sordid London scene[1] or even a sordid contemporary scene: it is what life in time is like compared with the fuller life the poet has felt. In this 'place of disaffection' there is neither the fulfilment which might have been experienced in the Garden, nor the 'way of negation' ('darkness to purify the soul'):

> Neither plenitude nor vacancy.

Eliot several times refers to the latter condition, which is called in *East Coker* 'the darkness of God'; and he describes it closely here and in the second part of the section. Another symbol for it, used in *Ash-Wednesday*, is aridity; St. John of the Cross called it the Dark Night of the Soul. It is a complete detachment in which, in the discipline of St. John, the religious is purified in readiness for the divine union—a discipline of contemplation beautifully described in the middle of the third section of *East Coker*.

In the second strophe Eliot does not hesitate even to play on words to drive home the meaning:

> Descend lower, descend only
> Into the world of perpetual solitude,
> World not world, but that which is not world, . . .

[1] Miss Helen Gardner (*op. cit.*) says that it is the London Tube. But the image is hinted, distorted and modified to render the meaning.

And there is a culminating emphasis in the echo of the second epigraph to the poem:

> This is the one way, and the other
> Is the same, . . .

The implication is that the 'descent' and the *Erhebung*, the 'way down' and the 'way up', are the same. The meaning of this is made clear by St. John of the Cross, writing on the 'ladder of contemplation':[1] 'Communications which are indeed of God have this property, that they humble the soul and at the same time exalt it. *For upon this road to go down is to go up, and to go up to go down;* for he that humbles himself is exalted and he that exalts himself is humbled.'

The next section is an imagined participation in this condition of detachment—death-in-life and life-in-death—with a glimpse, in a flash of light, of its goal. Here is the readiness, the 'waiting' in humility of *East Coker*, and a grateful acceptance of the Dark Night: the 'cloud' is now welcome as the 'cloud of unknowing'. The images are handled with the utmost tact as symbols of divine gifts which may be bestowed —but it is not in our power to draw them towards us. The sunflower may 'turn to us' as if an image of the divine light; the clematis (the Virgin's Bower, of blue, 'Mary's colour'[2]) may 'stray down, bend to us';

> Chill
> Fingers of yew be curled
> Down on us

conferring immortality. The effect of the passage depends on the way these movements—so much longed for, yet hardly expected—are suggested by a beautiful placing of verb, alliteration and assonance. The word 'chill' in isolation catches us unawares with a sudden suggestion of death, and perhaps of that spiritual aridity which St. John compares to the coolness of winter mornings. As a sudden contrast to these intimately felt 'hints and guesses' there is the remoteness and permanence of

> . . . the still point of the turning world

[1] *Dark Night*, II, xviii, 2. And see page 22.

[2] The Virgin's Bower is another name for the clematis. 'Mary's colour' is a quotation from *Ash-Wednesday*.

—with the brilliant flash of the kingfisher's wing as a fleeting hint of the keenness of the living ray.[1] The kingfisher is seen both as a creation of God, and as nothing compared with the life of its creator.

We can see in this short section the extraordinary resourcefulness of the spiritual exploration: a focusing of the whole personality on what it is beyond the power of the personality, unaided, to reach; a concentrated effort to gain every advantage in the patient struggle beyond appearance, the everyday world in which we are

> Distracted from distraction by distraction

towards a reality which, if not finite, may yet be glimpsed 'in the aspect of time'—

> Sudden in a shaft of sunlight.

Only a superficial reader could call this process 'quietism' even in its most tranquil stages. I have called it a patient struggle, but it is also a struggle to maintain patience:

> Words strain,
> Crack and sometimes break, under the burden, . . .
> Will not stay still. Shrieking voices
> Scolding, mocking, or merely chattering,
> Always assail them.

These lines and the last two lines of the poem remind us of the mood of the first part of Section III. But the fretful personality is put in its place:

> The Word in the desert
> Is most attacked by voices of temptation, . . .

The last two sentences of the first strophe of Section V have the macabre note of Harry's lines in *The Family Reunion*, but more restrained:

[1] After the kingfisher's wing
Has answered light to light, and is silent, . . .

Compare:
. . . *sì del cantare e sì del fiammeggiarsi*
luce con luce gaudiose e blande, . . . (*Paradiso*, XII. 23–4)

In and out, in an endless drift
Of shrieking forms in a circular desert . . .
(p. 107.)

The 'voices of temptation' are really impotent; they fade into:

The crying shadow in the funeral dance,
The loud lament of the disconsolate chimera.[1]

The monster is 'disconsolate', awaiting death: in any case it is unreal.

The first lines of the strophe elucidate the rest. Again the poet is contemplating the 'still point', and in the involution of the sentence beginning

Not the stillness of the violin, . . .

is lost in the infinity of the object of contemplation.

The last strophe begins with an allusion to the 'ladder of secret contemplation' of St. John of the Cross.[2] The concluding lines clearly place the vision of Section I and at the same time recall it (and incidentally, the opening of *A Song for Simeon*) vividly, as it is to be recalled vividly again in the succeeding poems. For these are not the writings of a mystic, but of a poet. There is no claim to *share* the experience of the saint. The purpose is awareness of the validity of that experience, of the reality of its goal, and of our place—nearer to the dust than to the sunlight, nearer to 'unbeing' than to 'being'—in the scale of reality. Helped by St. John of the Cross, and indirectly perhaps by St. Thomas Aquinas, but most of all by his own hard-won mastery over language, the poet is able to set down a statement which is apparently abstract, but which, backed by the rest of the poem, can stand as solid as stone:

Desire itself is movement
Not in itself desirable;
Love is itself unmoving,
Only the cause and end of movement, . . .

[1] *Chimera*: the Lycian monster killed by Bellerophon. Eliot takes advantage of the literal as well as the figurative sense of the word.

[2] See the *Dark Night*, Book II, Chapter XVII *et seq*. And compare the 'saints' stair' of *A Song for Simeon*. It is a figure for the soul's continual ascent and descent, or exaltation and humiliation, before it is finally united with God.

This, in its context, has the immovability of a hard fact which cannot be blasted, the scrupulously exact definition of a bracing truth. Man's limitations are seen to be greater than, in this age, it is usual to imagine them, but his *potentialities* are seen to be correspondingly higher.

> Sudden in a shaft of sunlight
> Even while the dust moves
> There rises the hidden laughter
> Of children in the foliage
> Quick now, here, now, always—

The last line quoted—with its initial suggestion of the darting of birds—beautifully expresses the exultation of the elusive moment of vision, and in its last word, the complete calm of the realization that the joy of the spiritual birth, the joy of the full 'consciousness' is *not in time.*

> Ridiculous the waste sad time
> Stretching before and after.

II

We might call the next Quartet 'Variations on a Theme of Mary, Queen of Scots'; for although the poem begins with an inversion of the theme, the motto stated in its original form at the end[1] informs and unifies the whole pattern. The statement with which the poem opens—

In my beginning is my end

—neatly condenses the personal implications of the first three lines of *Burnt Norton*. The comparison reminds us how much simpler in style *East Coker* is; but we must also remember that the lucidity is made possible by the exploratory labour which preceded it, by the 'speculation' of the previous poem. It crystallizes that speculation in a beautifully clear presentation of experience, personal and ancestral. What is realized in *Burnt Norton* is caught up into the pattern of *East Coker*, clarified, and developed.

Because knowledge derived from experience is so often untrustworthy—such, very briefly, is the argument of the poem—the only possible wisdom is humility. At a certain stage of spiritual progress, the soul must put itself into the hands of God; die in order to be born again. The dead past reminds us of the frailty and inadequacy of our own existence, but there is also a living past, and death is only a beginning. Present human life and achievement is negligible except in relation to the pattern of life of the whole race, and the soul will not progress in the human sphere; but with active fortitude and self-discipline the soul may reach 'into another intensity'.

Section I is a meditation on the village of East Coker, the Somerset home of Eliot's sixteenth-century ancestors. There is first a rapid sketch of the changing face of the village in the course of several centuries (Eliot's yew-tree growing in a few seconds): the telescoping of the passage of time that we notice in *Burnt Norton*, but here *visualized*, in a particular place. The strophe fades on an echo from *Ecclesiastes*[2] and a significant

[1] The motto actually embroidered by Mary Stuart was: *En ma fin est mon commencement.*

[2] The opening of Chapter iii.

close-up of the tattered arras in the manor house, shaken by the wind, its motto yet to be revealed. The beautifully rendered impression which follows, of the deep lane which

> insists on the direction
> Into the village, in the electric heat
> Hypnotized . . .

is more than a visualization of the scene. In the oppressive silence

> Wait for the early owl[1]

'those long since under earth' are vividly, compellingly there. The rhythm of the music and the dancing[2] of the Midsummer bonfire festivities seems to be caught up into the sustained movement of the passage; the comeliness and rightness of the old rustic culture are felt in the very rhythm of the verse:

> Keeping time,
> Keeping the rhythm in their dancing
> As in their living in the living seasons . . .

The rhythmic anaphora which follows pulses with life: this is not the voice that sadly echoes *Ecclesiastes* in the opening. Commentary, if commentary is needed, is provided by a recent essay by Mr. Eliot on another subject: what we have here is that 'insight into a harmony with nature which must be re-established if the truly Christian imagination is to be recovered by Christians'.

The rhythm slows to the meditative tempo of the opening: 'dung and death' recalls 'flesh, fur and fæces' in the first strophe. This is part of the pattern: village life, rooted in village tradition and the life of the countryside, the cycle of nature and the procession of the seasons. The vision fades, having reminded us that our remote past is more

[1] For the delicate note of foreboding in this, compare and contrast the line in *Murder in the Cathedral* (Fourth Edition, p. 53):

> The owl rehearses the hollow note of death.

And a friend points out that there is the same note in the dahlias: autumn is on us.

[2] According to Miss Helen Gardner (*op. cit.*), the sixteenth-century phrases woven into this passage are from Sir Thomas Elyot's *Boke named the Governour* (published in 1531). As Miss Gardner says, this allusion underlines the theme of personal ancestry in the poem.

Eliot uses *commodious* in the sense of 'fitting, convenient': Sir Thomas Elyot spoke of the 'dignitie and commoditie' of the marriage sacrament.

intimate to us than we imagine. 'But my beginning', the poet seems to be saying, 'is not just that'. What it is the infinity of the sea suggests:

> Out at sea the dawn wind
> Wrinkles and slides. I am here
> Or there, or elsewhere. In my beginning.

After *Burnt Norton* Eliot appears to have felt it necessary to come down to earth.[1] In *East Coker*, humility is not merely referred to: it informs the whole poem, as a resolute detachment from world and time and a search for words with which to express what is beyond world and time lie behind *Burnt Norton*. Corresponding to this difference, we have in the earlier poem an impressive tautness of control tending to rigidity, and in *East Coker* a flexibility of tone, pitch and tempo quite remarkable in a poem of its compactness and unity. Section II, for instance, has a deliberate 'false start'—an elaborate symbolic strophe heightened in pitch and tempo like a gramophone record played too quickly. The record stops; and there is a real voice speaking quietly, deliberately—at first a little wearily, but gathering urgency—a voice which compels attention. In the lines of Section I we had an enchanted whisper, close to the ear:

> In that open field
> If you do not come too close, if you do not come too close,
> On a summer midnight, you can hear . . .

Section II closes with the desolate echoes:

> The houses are all gone under the sea.
>
> The dancers are all gone under the hill.

This Quartet, we feel, cries out for performance.

[1] Contrast the rarefied allegorical vision in *Burnt Norton*, Section I and the immediate historical vision in the first section of *East Coker*. But the former is no less concrete in expressing a more remote feeling. And by Section III of *East Coker* the 'dancing' has become the Dantesque 'dance' of *Burnt Norton*, II.

Compare Brother George Every: 'It is the physical imagery that is important . . . in Eliot's later poetry. Religious feeling has to be translated in terms of physical sensation if it is to be made real again to those who are finding their way from a belief that only the physical is real to a renewed belief in the metaphysical. In their eyes the Christmas card stands for an old story, a kind of fiction, but El Greco gives a sense of interior experience, of something that tore at the very vitals of man' (*Christian Discrimination*, p. 59).

Section I is mainly about natural, Section II mainly about supernatural influence on the lives of persons. Birth is only the beginning of one's life on earth, not the beginning of one's way of life on earth: that beginning you may imagine in the historical past—in East Coker 'or elsewhere'. It is in this sense, partly, that

In my beginning is my end . . .

—which involves the realization, in humility, that one person in a single lifetime cannot change an ethos, and that one's ancestors—however fine their life—might say, like Eliot's Simeon:

I am dying in my own death and the deaths of those after me.

But that, we find, is not the whole meaning which the poem gives to its opening statement. 'In the middle way' one may be further from the true centre than in the beginning or the end: but what the beginning or the end—of one man or of mankind—is like can only be surmised by the kind of spiritual exploration that Eliot advocates and practises in these poems. If the beginning and the end are totally dissimilar human life is meaningless, for 'superficial notions of evolution' will not explain it. The belief that One Person *is* the 'beginning' and the 'end' is the belief to which these poems are directed; and *East Coker* implies at once the reality of the Alpha and Omega, and the position of man in relation to that reality, through a modification of the personal attitudes and assumptions, ambitions and fears—whether avowed or not—which direct our action and thought.

The argument of Section II has been very clearly summarized by Miss Helen Gardner:

'The lyrical passage with which the second movement opens contradicts both the rigid order and the stillness of the first. The idea of pattern is rejected, but so is the idea of peace. The seasons are all disordered . . . the flowers of high summer jostle those of Spring and Winter. There is war too among the constellations, ending with the apocalyptic vision of the end of the world, burnt out to an icy cinder.

> But this romantic vision of chaos the poet rejects, for a plain, almost prosaic statement of the same chaos in the life of the individual. There, too, we find no ordered sequence, pattern or development. The metaphor of autumnal serenity is false applied to man; experience does not bring wisdom, nor old age peace. The time when one knows never arrives, and the pattern is falsified by every new moment. . . . As we try to hold the past, it slips from us, engulfed in the darkness of the present' (*op. cit.*, p. 90).

The lucid exposition is only broken in one sentence, which renders in the dislocation of its syntax and the potency of its imagery the supernatural environment of which men of the world are oblivious:

> In the middle, not only in the middle of the way
> But all the way, in a dark wood, in a bramble,
> On the edge of a grimpen, where is no secure foothold,
> And menaced by monsters, fancy lights,
> Risking enchantment.

There is for a moment a quickening of the pulse, a disturbance of the breathing suggested in the verse rhythm—a direct poetic impact. The verse echoes itself, and echoes too *nel mezzo del cammin* . . . and *per una selva oscura* of the opening of the *Inferno*. And before this vision of the soul in constant perplexity and danger we have a sentence reminiscent of that passage of tortuous cerebration in the middle of *Gerontion* ('Think now . . .'), but here we are given the result of experience rather than—in the manner of Jacobean verse—the dramatic stress and strain of thought.

Rising out of this experience is the realization of the 'wisdom of humility' in which the section culminates:

> Do not let me hear
> Of the wisdom of old men, but rather of their folly,
> Their fear of fear and frenzy, their fear of possession,
> Of belonging to another, or to others, or to God.
> The only wisdom we can hope to acquire
> Is the wisdom of humility: humility is endless.

And the episode closes with echoes from Section I which express the transience of human life and culture.

It is unnecessary, in reading Section III, to remember that the opening lines contain three phrases adapted from the first speech of *Samson Agonistes*;[1] more relevant is Eliot's debt to St. John of the Cross, though a student of that saint will not necessarily be more responsive to Eliot's verse than a sensitive reader who has never heard of him. I shall, however, provide a few signposts for the puzzled reader by referring to certain passages from St. John, since at least one reader has found them helpful.

Here is the first:

> 'I see that Christ is known very little by those who consider themselves His friends: for we see them seeking their own pleasures and consolations in Him because of their great love for themselves, but not loving His bitter trials and His death because of their great love for Him. *I am speaking now of those who consider themselves His friends; for such as live far away, withdrawn from Him, great men of letters and of influence, and all others who live yonder, with the world, and are eager about their ambitions and their prelacies, may be said not to know Christ; and their end, however good, will be very bitter.* Of such I make no mention in these lines; but mention will be made of them on the day of judgement, for to them it was necessary to speak first this word of God, as to those whom God set up as guides, by reason of their learning and their high position' (*Ascent*, II, vii, 12).

This passage, together with *Revelation*, vi. 12–15, will illuminate the opening of Section III more than any commentary of mine. For the rest, what is required is inclination rather than explanation.[2]

[1] See lines 80, 86–7 and 89 of that poem. There is in Eliot's *Note on the Verse of John Milton* (1936)—extracts from which are reprinted in the Penguin collection, *The Poets and their Critics* (ed. Hugh Sykes Davies)—a critical observation which may well have led him to improve (in more than one sense) Milton's phrase, *vacant interlunar cave*. 'Milton does not infuse new life into the word, as Shakespeare does', he wrote. '*Interlunar* is certainly a stroke of genius, but is merely combined with "vacant" and "cave", rather than giving and receiving life from them . . .' We see from this small example how much critical intelligence and poetic imagination is involved in Eliot's use of earlier poetry. It is frequently, as we see in other instances, a way of making us conscious of the presence of the past, and his views on tradition in literature are significantly implied in the conclusion of this poem.

[2] I owe this phrase to a comment of Rilke's on his *Sonnets to Orpheus*, quoted by Mr. D. J. Enright.

Eliot, from the start, *achieves* his attitude of alert detachment in the characteristic contrast:

> And dark the Sun and Moon, and the Almanach de Gotha
> And the Stock Exchange Gazette, the Directory of Directors . . .

Milton is indeed transformed!

In the lines:

> And we all go with them, into the silent funeral,
> Nobody's funeral, for there is no one to bury . . .

as in the line of *The Dry Salvages*,

> (And the time of death is every moment)

the poet calmly reveals an abyss beneath our feet.

The theme of these opening lines, then, is not merely physical death, but the darkness and destruction of the Last Judgement. The 'motive of action' of the worldly is lost because it was worldly and temporal: those who have forgotten their true *raison d'être* cease to *be*. Therefore there is *no one* to bury. But the lines do not only apply to the worldly. St. John teaches us that that which is created is as *nothing* compared with the Creator. After the apparent spiritual death, the emptiness and aridity of the Dark Night of the Soul, there may be rebirth:

> . . . let the dark come upon you
> Which shall be the darkness of God.

There is here a transition from the utter deprivation and blindness of the 'dark' of the first nine lines to the 'darkness' of the rest of the section, the darkness which is a stage of purgation in the soul's progress. The fullness of meaning of the last line quoted is best indicated by the following clear commentary of St. John, in which he is elucidating the symbol used in his own *Mystic Stanzas:*

'We may say that there are three reasons for which this passage made by the soul to union with God is called night.

The first has to do with the point from which the soul goes forth, for it has gradually to deprive itself of desire for all worldly things which it possessed, by denying them to itself; the which denial and deprivation are, as it were, night to all the senses of man. The second reason has to do with the mean or the road along which the soul must travel to this union—that is, faith, which is likewise as dark as night to the understanding. The third has to do with the point to which it travels—namely God, who, equally, is dark night to the soul in this life . . .' (*Ascent*, I. ii. 1).

I have already implied that Eliot is not merely saying, in a brilliant verse paraphrase, what St. John has already said in clear prose. You may call the three beautiful similes which follow 'illuminating'; but you need to add that they are—without being *illogical*—rather different from logical analogies. Lines like these:

> . . . as, when an underground train, in the tube, stops too long between stations
> And the conversation rises and slowly fades into silence
> And you see behind every face the mental emptiness deepen
> Leaving only the growing terror of nothing to think about;
> Or when, under ether, the mind is conscious but conscious of nothing—

freeze the thought and feeling into a form, give that shock of heightened awareness which prose cannot give without becoming poetry. The kind of *contrast* which you find here between the two terms of each comparison is itself evidence of a fine poetic imagination. I have said before that the poet is not claiming the experience of the saint: the often quoted lines which follow[1] embody the 'wisdom of humility'. Although the movement of the poem is from the life of the senses to the life of the spirit, from meditation to contemplation, it remains a *poem*. The expression of the 'awareness' depends on imagery, on sense perception; the sensibility is disciplined, not mortified:

[1] For the *thought* of these lines, compare St. John of the Cross: *The Dark Night of the Soul*, I. x. 4.

Whisper of running streams, and winter lightning,
The wild thyme unseen and the wild strawberry,
The laughter in the garden, echoed ecstasy
Not lost, but requiring, pointing to the agony
Of death and birth.

These last lines might have been developed from St. John:

'The will of the soul is not lost but becomes the will of God' (*Spiritual Canticle*, XXXVII. 2).

If so, the idea is transformed. The haunting rhythmic anaphora of the previous lines, the sudden overwhelming *débordement* of imagery are as direct as music. How much of 'ecstasy' is echoed in the images we realize if we remember *Marina* and the first movement of *Burnt Norton.* They suggest the moments of illumination in the flux of time which are assurances of a reality that conquers the flux. The theme of rebirth which is stated in the *Journey of the Magi*, *A Song for Simeon* and elsewhere and which is repeated in the motto at the end of the poem, provides the transition, here, to the last strophe.

To arrive where you are, to get from where you are not, is a re-statement of the theme.

The images recede, and the section ends with an austere exhortation, consisting of Eliot's version of six lines from *The Ascent of Mount Carmel*, I. xiii. 11, introduced by five lines and developed in three of his own. This sudden transition to a severe abstractness of statement and a *jeu de paradoxes* almost as grave as the biblical paronomasia on the name of Peter is a superbly calculated effect. The difference between the 'temporal' and the 'eternal' is expressed in phrases which are condensed to the utmost: the simplification of expression which you find in a biblical phrase like 'before Abraham was, *I am*' is carried a stage further by means of a play on two senses of the verb 'to be'.

In order to arrive there,
To arrive *where you are* . . .

is Eliot's adaptation of St. John's phrase, 'In order to arrive at being everything'—in other words, at complete realization of one's potentialities, which *in time* are always in process of being realized. If you take the phrase 'where you are' in the common sense ('where you are placed at the moment')—as you do at a first reading—the whole line appears unintelligible. And the process of finding a meaning for the line is not merely the process of solving a puzzle: it involves changing, in a moment, the direction of the whole mind, which is perhaps influenced more than we imagine by common forms of speech. As the eye may be first focused on a fly on the window-pane and then, immediately, on a distant mountain, so the mind in grasping the line first makes the too familiar assumption of movement in time, and then in a flash realizes the intended concept of *being*. The poetic effect of *surprise* which drives home the meaning is gained not through two successive statements, but through two successive responses to one statement. (And even if we do not get further than the first response, we get as far as the line of the Chorus in *The Family Reunion* will take us:

> We do not like to walk out of a door, and find ourselves
> back in the same room.[1])

A study of St. John of the Cross is outside the scope of this essay; but readers who cannot follow the sense of the remainder of this strophe will, I think, find their immediate difficulties removed by the second paragraph of the passage from Aquinas which I quoted earlier.[2] The last line, which may still puzzle some readers even after they have studied Eliot's source, has two meanings: (i) 'this life is as nothing compared with perfect being'; (ii) 'the condition of complete spiritual humility, "emptiness", "nothingness" (or St. John's "Dark Night") is necessary if you are to achieve the fullest being in this life'.

In the next section Eliot has revived, revitalized a traditional form—the 'metaphysical poem'. It is no mere imitation of Donne or another; it is as alive to us to-day, as vitally related to contemporary speech and conditions of thought as Donne's *Holy Sonnets* were to his contemporaries. Eliot uses the poetic paradox and the 'conceit' of Donne and his followers; but the symbolism—as the reader realizes at once—is of a kind quite

[1] *op. cit.*, p. 132. [2] See p. 16.

distinct from that of early seventeenth-century poetry. I will suggest briefly an interpretation of this symbolism, and then comment on its effect.

Clearly, as the last line indicates, this is a poem for Good Friday;[1] there can be no doubt, then, about the identity of the *wounded surgeon.* The development of this symbol in the first stanza realizes afresh the significance of the Redemption.

Our only health is the disease . . .

This paradox indicates the following connected senses for *the disease:* (i) Suffering as a means of grace—*i.e.* a physical evil regarded as a spiritual good (this is the *enigma of the fever chart*). *Adam's curse* is incessant toil and suffering. (ii) *Necessary* evils (compare 'Sin is Behovely' in *Little Gidding*). To be *wholly* preoccupied with resisting evils may be itself evil: Faith, Hope, Love demand other preoccupations leading to positive good. The *dying nurse* is, presumably, the Church Militant.

. . . to be restored, our sickness must grow worse.

(Compare: 'In my end is my beginning.') The only release from pain is death, and we must accept purgation as a release from evil.

The whole earth is our hospital
Endowed by the ruined millionaire, . . .

The image of the *hospital* occurs in *The Family Reunion*:

Up and down, through the stone passages
Of an immense and empty hospital . . .
Up and down. Until the chain breaks.
(pp. 107–8.)

—there used to convey Agatha's sense of confinement in world and time. The *ruined millionaire* is Adam.[2] It is true that a millionaire is not likely to be completely ruined spiritually if he is benevolent enough to endow a hospital: but as the

[1] *East Coker* was written for Good Friday, 1940.

[2] I originally thought that the *ruined millionaire* was the Fallen Angel. I am indebted to Mr. Eliot for the correction.

endowment in question included Original Sin, it was not wholly charitable. And but for the ruined millionaire, the *surgeon* would not have visited the hospital—would not have been its leading patient, suffering the greatest pain without alleviation (*My God, my God, why hast thou forsaken me?*).

> . . . *the absolute paternal care*
> *That will not leave us, but prevents us everywhere.*

'Prevents' is of course used in the seventeenth-century sense which has survived in the Prayer Book—the first of the following senses: (i) '(*of God*) to go before with spiritual guidance and help, or *to predispose to repentance*, faith, and good works'; (ii) 'to balk or baffle by precautionary measures' (O.E.D.). The second sense is also present, suggesting physical frustration ending in the immobility of death, which is the starting point of the next, and climactic stanza. The following extract from an essay of Eliot published in *The Tyro* (1922) and quoted by Matthiessen provides an excellent comment on the achievement of language in the last line quoted:

> 'Whatever words a writer employs, he benefits by knowing as much as possible of the history of those words, of the uses to which they have already been applied. Such knowledge facilitates his task of giving to the word a new life and to the language a new idiom. The essential of tradition is this: in getting as much as possible of the whole weight of the history of the language behind his word.'

This is not a defence of pedantry in literature: what Mr. Eliot meant is shown in the life of his verse.

> . . . *frigid purgatorial fires*
> *Of which the flame is roses*, . . .

The *rose* is the emblem of human love, becoming divine; the emblem of the martyr; the emblem of Christ's love (the Five Wounds were symbolized by a five-petalled red rose). The exquisite clashes of symbolism in these lines suggest the exquisite pain of purgation which is desired.

All this is of course mere annotation; but the consummate art of the verse speaks for itself:

. . . if we do well, we shall
Die of the absolute paternal care . . .

The last stanza has that very *serious* wit which has rarely been achieved since the seventeenth century. You find it, for instance—to take an example from a poet whose personality is completely different from Eliot's—in Herbert's couplet:

Love is that liquor sweet and most divine
Which my God feels as blood, but I as wine.

(Eliot also refers to the Eucharist, but that is not my only reason for quoting the lines.) Eliot's wit is more intense, the jaw muscles are tighter. Unlike Herbert's, it is almost satirical—it *smarts.* But the quotation serves to show how much Eliot is in contact with the seventeenth-century tradition of English devotional verse. His lines are closer in feeling to Herbert's than to his own lines in *The Hippopotamus* which he appears to echo. The wit of *The Hippopotamus* is in comparison jocose. The wit of this last stanza not only clears the air of religiose sentiment—as did the wit of the earlier poem; it heightens the devotional feeling to the utmost.

If we consider the effect of the symbolism in the whole section, there seems to be a tension between the 'sense' which each reader makes out for himself as he reads, and the pattern of symbols; and this tension of feeling is increased by rhyme, rhythm, and a concentration of expression tending to 'conceits' and paradox. What Yeats said of rhythm in poetry applies to the whole form of Eliot's poem (for the section is a poem in itself): its purpose is *to prolong the moment of contemplation.*

We turn from these taut, beautifully formed stanzas to 'free' verse with the tone of the second strophe of Section II. The poet begins with a personal confession, a consciousness of inadequacy, and works up to an impersonal and impassioned climax. (We remember: 'humility is endless.') We are reminded of the opening of the poem; we are back in East Coker ('or elsewhere'):

Home is where one starts from. . . .

The line

There is a time for the evening under starlight, . . .

recalls in its context the echoes of *Ecclesiastes* and the setting of the vision in Section I; but what we heard 'on a summer midnight' seems no stranger, now, than

> the evening under lamplight
> (The evening with the photograph album).

The poet is conveying his sense of the presence of the past; and the two previous sentences hark back to the groping speculations on time at the opening of *Burnt Norton*, and point forward to their further development in Section II of *The Dry Salvages* and in the conclusion of the sequence. Both

> Love is itself unmoving, . . .
>
> *Burnt Norton*

and

> Love is most nearly itself
> When here and now cease to matter
>
> *East Coker*

prepare us for *Little Gidding*. (The thought is again in line with St. John of the Cross: 'Love consists not in feeling great things, but *in having great detachment* and in suffering for the Beloved.') And the reference in

> We must be still and still moving . . .

does not need pointing out. The superb imagery of these concluding lines—a preparation for the opening of *The Dry Salvages*—has that telling immediacy which is characteristic of the whole poem, and which will help many readers to understand the more remote *Burnt Norton*.

III

If, in order to grasp the comprehensiveness of the series, we attempt to define the aim and method of the author in each of the four poems, we inevitably leave out of account just those elements in the separate members which bind them into a unity; but a detailed examination of the poems constantly reminds us of the significant recurrence of imagery and theme. In *Burnt Norton*, considered as a unit of contemplation, we see the effort to apprehend complete reality, complete being, and the medium of that being, which are glimpsed in moments of insight in the medium of time. If *Burnt Norton* is primarily concerned with the object, *East Coker* is primarily concerned with the subject—with personal experience, with the validity of personal experience, and with personal salvation. Now we are transported from the English village to the American coastline of *The Dry Salvages*. And with the change of setting from the village to the sea there is a shift of mental perspective from the person and the family—personal experience and inheritance—to the race, and to that in and about men which men 'choose to forget'; from the telescoping of the time sequence to

> the trailing
> Consequence of further days and hours, . . .

The tone becomes more distant, more impersonal—the reader is not to be taken by the arm this time—the expression more expansive; and the symbolism carries the weight of nearly the whole of the poem.

And from the first section we are amazed at the weight the symbol does carry. From the modest beginning the lines proceed to a development of immense controlled power and sonority; the surge of the 'ground swell' is beneath the rhythm of the lines, the 'granite teeth' in the very texture of the words:

> The sea howl
> And the sea yelp, are different voices
> Often together heard: the whine in the rigging,
> The menace and caress of wave that breaks on water,

The distant rote in the granite teeth,
And the wailing warning from the approaching headland
Are all sea voices, and the heaving groaner
Rounded homewards, and the seagull.
And under the oppression of the silent fog
The tolling bell
Measures time not our time, rung by the unhurried
Ground swell, a time
Older than the time of chronometers, older . . .

Our everyday routine world appears to be drowned; this first section and the following stanzas include it, but also distance it—include too so much of which, as we are involved in the process described, we become unconscious. Numbed by organized routine lives, we awake to the reality, a waste and vastness more terrifying than as we live in it we conceive it to be—and not only this, but a deeper reality: the old terror of the 'undiscovered country' revived in the terror of the forgotten sea. Instead of *my beginning* there is *the beginning*, but not yet *the end*—though that is hinted in the closing lines of the movement. We should note this development and promise of development, but note too that 'the beginning' is here prehistoric, prehuman, that the primitive note of the opening is no accident. The main theme of the movement is stated in the reflection of Section II:

> The backward look behind the assurance
> Of recorded history, the backward half-look
> Over the shoulder, towards the primitive terror.

The opening evokes an elemental animism, a pristine religion; the river[1] is seen as a 'strong brown god',

> . . . Unhonoured, unpropitiated
> By worshippers of the machine, but waiting, watching and waiting.

Without any direct reference to *super*natural power the poet exposes man's weakness, his pitiable blindness to natural forces *in him* and about him which he cannot subdue and which he ignores at his own peril; dissolves the arrogance of a machine

[1] Mr. Eliot says that he had in mind the Mississippi.

age boasting control over nature; suggests a non-human power in the immensity of a creation apparently dwarfing man, and in the potent evocation of a time 'not our time':

> a time
> Older than the time of chronometers, older
> Than time counted by anxious worried women
> Lying awake, calculating the future,
> Trying to unweave, unwind, unravel
> And piece together the past and the future, . . .

We can regulate our watches, but this rhythm of creation and destruction we can neither regulate nor predict.

Section II opens with a concentrated expression of this rhythm, a movement so endless and inescapable that it has the horrible fascination of a vortex which we are not sure is in motion and whose cause and purpose we cannot fathom. The form—the rhyme-scheme—of this passage is so directly evocative that we are hardly conscious of its ingenuity. The passage *appears* to be an expression of profound despair and fatalism, as if continued existence in this 'time' were felt as an intolerable stagnation ('Ridiculous the waste sad time . . .') —a movement which as the verse form suggests is not movement, because moving to no goal. But even while the poet builds this castle of despair, he shows us that there is only sand to build it on: for the theme of the Annunciation, hinted in the first stanza, is echoed antiphonally in the stanzas which follow and directly stated—*breathed*—in the last:

> . . . Only the hardly, barely prayable
> Prayer of the one Annunciation.

And Miss Helen Gardner's comment on this part of the poem is helpful:

> 'Under the metaphor of fishermen setting out on their perilous voyages, over "an ocean littered with wastage", it pictures the lives of individual men, the sum of which makes history. It finds meaning in the process only in the union of the temporal with the eternal, in annunciations: the calamitous annunciation of terror and danger, the last annunciation of death, and the one Annunciation of history.

The only *end* to the flux of history is man's response to the eternal' (*op. cit.*, p. 93).

There is a hint in the third stanza of the 'detachment from self . . .' to which Section II of *Little Gidding* leads; and in the fifth stanza Eliot, using his symbol, universalizes the personal statement he made at the beginning of the last section of *East Coker*:

> . . . perhaps neither gain nor loss.
> For us, there is only the trying. . . .

Eliot spoke in *East Coker* of the fear of 'belonging . . . to God'. He has, in these two or three pages, directed an immense imaginative power and subtlety of poetic resource towards undermining this fear by means of fundamental human terrors, the reality of which we cannot gainsay. And after this, there is the calm voice summing up—and what concentrated attention it commands! Those who, on reading

> It seems, as one becomes older,
> That the past has another pattern, and ceases to be a mere sequence——
> Or even development: the latter a partial fallacy
> Encouraged by superficial notions of evolution
> Which becomes, in the popular mind, a means of disowning the past. . . .

feel moved to tear the passage from its context and exclaim that this is not poetry, are ignoring the effect that is gained in a long poem by contrasting degrees of intensity in its parts—ignoring the effect that is gained most strikingly, here, from such contrast. But to the reader who is attending, if Beethoven reached beyond music in his last Quartets, Eliot reaches beyond poetry in these poems.[1] Such a reader can understand the statement in *East Coker* that 'the poetry does not matter', even while as he reads he is profoundly thankful for it. And there is more art in the verse of this strophe than a first glance might suggest.

[1] In an unpublished lecture quoted on pp. 89–90 of Matthiessen's book, *The Achievement of T. S. Eliot*, Mr. Eliot used this comparison in stating his aims as a poet. Perhaps it is no accident that the association is prompted by his title, *Four Quartets*.

In the opening of the section we felt time as a process of incessant change and dissolution which yet seems to include certain elements which remain undissolved. Now the attention is directed, calmly and unemotionally, to these elements as they are revealed first of all in personal experience. We remember

> Only through time time is conquered. . .

and now follow and are developed some of the

> hints and guesses,
> Hints followed by guesses . . .

—hints in time which point to a medium beyond time. The 'waste sad time stretching before and after' is no longer felt as 'ridiculous', but is the object of patient observation, patient induction; to this extent is *The Dry Salvages* complementary to *Burnt Norton*. The popular mind 'disowning the past', desiring change for change's sake, escapes all of reality but the small fraction of it that we are forced to face. Looking beyond that small fraction we see that

> Time the destroyer is time the preserver, . . .

A momentary ellipsis, a precarious hanging on to the word 'meaning' disturbs the regularity of the syntax at the recollection of the illuminating moment of *Burnt Norton:*

> The moments of happiness—not the sense of well-being,
> Fruition, fulfilment, security or affection,
> Or even a very good dinner, but the sudden illumination—
> We had the experience but missed the meaning,
> And approach to the meaning restores the experience
> In a different form, beyond any meaning
> We can assign to happiness.

We see how, just as the genial touch in that third line throws into relief its closing phrase, the plain conversational reflection of the previous sentence makes us sensitive to the intensification of plain speech in the quotation. In the first lines the verse breaks, and rising on its crest is the *sudden illumination*—the moment of infinite significance just caught, like the flash of the kingfisher's wing, in the flow of time. But the calm reflection persists: the nearer we get to the meaning of the experience the more we realize—as in *Burnt Norton*, Section II—that for its completion outside time happiness is too weak a word: flesh can no more endure heaven than it can endure damnation.

This, then, is one moment that time preserves, and the inclusiveness of the meaning of that moment is suggested as the poet develops the lines in *East Coker* to which I have already referred:

Not the intense moment
Isolated, with no before and after,
But a lifetime burning in every moment
And not the lifetime of one man only
But of old stones that cannot be deciphered.

As the poet has hinted at an eternal joy in contemplation, so he now hints, perhaps, at an eternal torment in the 'moments of agony' which

are likewise permanent
With such permanence as time has. . . .
People change, and smile: but the agony abides.

And the section closes with a climactic development of the symbolism of Section I:

Time the destroyer is time the preserver,
Like the river with its cargo of dead negroes, cows and chicken coops,
The bitter apple and the bite in the apple. . . .

The allusion to the Fall in that surprising, incisive third line is given extra emphasis by the method of *contrast* we noted before. The comparison is a simple one: that of the river of time bearing with it evidence of man's sin (the *dead negroes*) and man's innate evil (the *bitter apple*). But what force Eliot gives it by his quiet understatement! The remaining lines of the section express with extraordinary power the certainty of a permanent purpose and reality—a terrifying reality—behind the flux of time and apparent drift and turbulence of history.

In the third section, new strategy is used to gain the next stage. The approach is by way of the *Bhagavad-Gita* ('The Song of the Blessed'), the sacred Indian poem regarded by Hindus as a rival of the New Testament. In it Arjuna is required to engage in battle against a hostile but related clan; but at the sight of his near relatives in the opposing army he hesitates to begin the fight, and is recalled to a sense of duty by Krishna, who stands beside him as his charioteer. Krishna reveals himself as an incarnation of the one God. The way of salvation, he says, lies in action performed in fulfilment of duty, but action performed in such complete freedom from personal desires or interests that it is equivalent to the abstention from action of the contemplative life. Such action frees the actor from continued worldly existence, if he thinks not of the 'fruit of action' but of God. Eliot's quotation is completed in the *Gita* as follows:

> 'On whatever sphere of being the mind of man may be intent at the time of death, to that he goes . . . having been used to ponder on it. Therefore at all times remember me; and engage in battle.'

The first lines of the section express in fresh metaphor that telescoping of the time sequence with which we are now familiar, but that is not all they express. The last section implied a unity behind the changing manifestations of time, and this unity and its significance are now brought out in another aspect. It is a unity which is insisted on not only in *Ecclesiastes* and in the speeches of Krishna in the *Bhagavad-Gita*, but also in the writings of the pre-Socratic philosopher who is quoted in the epigraphs to *Burnt Norton*. The sixth line is an adaptation of the second of these epigraphs, which can be related to Eliot's lines in *Burnt Norton* and elsewhere on the 'beginning' and the 'end', and to Heraclitus's own analogy, that '(in rotation) the beginning and the end are common':[1]

[1] Diels: *Die Fragmente der Vorsokratiker* (Herakleitos), Fr. 103. It is possible, but misleading, to relate Eliot's line to what Diels tells us is the Heraclitean doctrine—creation by, and proportionate dissolution into, the one Logos, identified with Fire; and even to Krishna's doctrine of metempsychosis. But the poet is only interested in Heraclitus and the *Bhagavad-Gita* in so far as they reveal to him different ways of putting the same thing, different aspects of the truth; and a study of these sources beyond a certain point does not illuminate Eliot's poetry.

And the way up is the way down, the way forward is the way back.

That statement sums up what we have seen in the opening lines. The 'book that has never been opened' is perhaps a reminiscence of the last canto of the *Paradiso*, the moment of the Divine vision:

> *Nel suo profondo vidi che s'interna,*
> *legato con amore in un volume,*
> *ciò che per l'universo si squaderna; . . .*

('Within its depths I saw ingathered, bound by love in one volume, the scattered leaves of the universe.')

And the line I have quoted implies that all life returns to its source and is included in its source, and that you cannot escape from this ultimate reality. It is this which perplexed the Chorus in *The Family Reunion:*

> We do not like to climb a stair, and find that it takes us down. . . .
> . . . what is being done to us?
>
> (pp. 132–3.)

Herbert Read once said that the function of art is to stretch the mind beyond the limits of the understanding; and you cannot explain what is beyond the limits of the understanding. Here we can only bring ourselves to the point at which we are capable of *taking* the line: and if you remember what has gone before, you find that the poet has already brought you to that point. Re-read, for instance, the second strophe of *Burnt Norton*, Section III, and you find that the first half of the line—which is the difficult half—becomes clearer.

I now give three quotations in order to bring out the meaning of the middle one, which follows the lines we have been considering:

> People change, and smile: but the agony abides.
>
> (Section II)
>
> . . . time is no healer: the patient is no longer here.
>
> (Section III)

Fare forward, travellers! . . .
You are not the same people who left that station
Or who will arrive at any terminus, . . .

(Section III)

The symbolism and dramatic setting make an immediate impression and more than anything else help us to realize the meaning. The *patient*, the person who suffers, has 'left the station': and the faces of the travellers, of whom he is one, 'relax from grief into relief'. He is detached from action and suffering, and no longer conscious of time: 'time is withdrawn'. In this condition he is able to see that 'the time of death is every moment', for if death is an entry into eternity, the awareness of eternity—the detachment from time—is like death. And this is precisely what Krishna says in the *Bhagavad-Gita*—that the state of detachment which should accompany the active life is like 'leaving the body and departing from this world'. So the fullest life is, as we are told in the last section,

. . . in a lifetime's death in love, . . .

—the life of the saint, striving for complete being, which is not in time, not in this world.

That crucial parenthesis—

(And the time of death is every moment) [1]

includes the reflection of *East Coker:*

. . . the pattern is new in every moment . . .

and carries it a stage further. And the theme is taken up again in *Little Gidding:*

[1] In effect, Eliot here condenses into a single line of great power the passage of *Murder in the Cathedral:*

What is the day that we know that we hope for or fear for?
Every day is the day we should fear from or hope from. One moment
Weighs like another. Only in retrospection, selection,
We say, that was the day. The critical moment
That is always now, and here. Even now, in sordid particulars
The eternal design may appear.

(*op. cit.* p. 57.)

Every phrase and every sentence is an end and a beginning,
Every poem an epitaph. And any action
Is a step to the block, to the fire, down the sea's throat
Or to an illegible stone: and that is where we start.

The luminous invocation to the Virgin which forms the next section is thrown into relief by what precedes it, and by its own brevity and restraint. More impersonal, more self-sufficient, less obviously rich in poignant association than the invocation in *Ash-Wednesday*, it bears in its clarity a weight of implication which leads us to perceive unsuspected depths in an apparently simple, formal prayer. There is not only the adaption of half a line from the prayer of St. Bernard in the *Paradiso*[1]—so much more than a literary allusion—as a suggestion of these depths; the reference to the 'anxious worried women' and the fishermen of the earlier part of the poem—the *contrast* between those earlier passages and the present one—makes us realize the development of attitude in the poem to one of resignation, humility and faith, which has come of facing the agony of existence. The clang of the sea-bell, before associated with the terrors of an implacable natural force and movement, now becomes an angelus. In one sense the world no longer seems alien, inhuman; in another—that of Krishna's injunction in Section III—life in the world is only a brief transit in which labour (like the fishermen's) is necessary but 'results' are vain—in which

right action is freedom
From past and future also.

But let us look at the beginning of this last section. The reminder of the Angel's message to Mary in the last line of Section IV is a preparation for the concluding statement on the theme of the Incarnation. To make way for divinity, divination is first rejected—divination from the Etruscan haruspex to Mr. Naylor. (This is, of course, a development

[1] *Paradiso*, XXXIII. 1. *Vergine madre, figlia del tuo figlio . . .*
Virgin mother, daughter of thine own son.
And Eliot's next line was possibly suggested by l. 100 of Canto XXXI.

from Section I.) Then follows the lucid, positive statement which clarifies so many of the complexities of the three poems we have considered:

> Men's curiosity searches past and future
> And clings to that dimension. But to apprehend
> The point of intersection of the timeless
> With time, is an occupation for the saint—
> No occupation either, but something given
> And taken, in a lifetime's death in love,
> Ardour and selflessness and self-surrender.
> For most of us, there is only the unattended
> Moment, the moment in and out of time,
> The distraction fit, lost in a shaft of sunlight,
> The wild thyme unseen, or the winter lightning
> Or the waterfall, or music heard so deeply
> That it is not heard at all, but you are the music
> While the music lasts. These are only hints and guesses,
> Hints followed by guesses; and the rest
> Is prayer, observance, discipline, thought and action.
> The hint half guessed, the gift half understood, is Incarnation.

There is no need for me to rehearse the relations of imagery and theme between this masterly recapitulation and previous key-passages. What I wish to stress is that the achievement of simplicity and precision in this statement of belief can only be appreciated as a development of the poetic and spiritual discipline involved in all and more than we have considered. It is in a sense the reward of all the patient metaphysical searching, the following of the way of negation, the facing of the 'primitive terror'—for all that involved more than imagination and intellect—and as much a raid on the incredible as a 'raid on the inarticulate'. In another sense it is only the reward of the struggle with words, and so—if I may use Eliot's own phrasing—a beginning as well as an end.

And, of course, the recapitulation involves more than selection and repetition, and more than being explicit. A phrase like 'the point of intersection of the timeless with time' looks deceptively easy—because Eliot has found it for us. But to arrive at the phrase *and* to arrive at its meaning, is not so easy; and it is not surprising that once Eliot had, so to speak, held on to it, he did not let go.[1]

Following 'Incarnation', we have:

> Here the impossible union
> Of spheres of existence is actual,
> Here the past and future
> Are conquered, and reconciled, . . .

Here the annotator might busy himself with references to (say) Nicholas of Cusa's doctrine of the 'concordance of contraries'; but what really matters is the reference *within* the poems. It is essential to see how Eliot reached this point; and we are closer to understanding not only if we can see the relation between these lines and the rest of the poem, but if we can see them as a development of the last strophe of *Burnt Norton*, II, and of the symbolism, 'conceits' and paradoxes of *East Coker*, IV; and if we can see what they add to the conclusion of the first poem. As we read the remainder of the sentence we have a new insight into the meaning of the first and second sections of the present poem, in which the 'dæmonic, chthonic powers' were suggested in the menace of the waters, the 'drifting wreckage' and 'the river with its cargo of dead negroes. . . .' And when we come to the final sentence we realize how much more than autobiographical reflection were those lines in *East Coker:*

> There is only the fight to recover what has been lost
> And found and lost again and again: and now, under conditions
> That seem unpropitious. But perhaps neither gain nor loss.
> For us, there is only the trying. The rest is not our business.
>
> *East Coker*, V.

> For most of us, this is the aim
> Never here to be realized;
> Who are only undefeated
> Because we have gone on trying; . . .
>
> *The Dry Salvages*, V.

[1] See *Little Gidding:*
. . . the intersection of the timeless moment . . .

'. . . Never here to be realized'; but we shall not forget how much of the 'trying' there is in the whole sequence—trying from 'here', from living perception. Those who think that this last section saves them the trouble of reading what has gone before, are taking the bare bones, not the body of the lines. The phrase 'temporal reversion' is not just a *recherché* equivalent for 'return to dust', or for one's earthly remains; it connects the statement with the poet's constant struggle to reach, through time, that which is before time. Our bondage to nature—so powerfully presented at the beginning of the poem—ends with physical dissolution, which can now be faced calmly:

> We, content at the last
> If our temporal reversion nourish
> (Not too far from the yew-tree)
> The life of significant soil.

This recalls the ancient rustics of East Coker, who are now 'nourishing the corn'. The 'yew-tree' suggests sanctified ground, and 'significant soil' perhaps hints at the 'symbol perfected in death' of the third section of *Little Gidding*, which gives us more than we could see for ourselves in the word *tradition*. But the emphasis in these lines is on the *rightness* of death.

> (— that is the one action . . .
> Which should fructify in the lives of others:
> And do not think of the fruit of action.)

The Dry Salvages begins with what looks like the pagan vision, and ends with the Christian.

IV

WE might expect from a lesser poet a static conclusion to the sequence; but *Little Gidding* is in its different way (what variety there is in *Four Quartets*!) as intense a poem as any of the others. It is no more facilely tranquil than is *Burnt Norton.* The power of the poem seems, as we consider the whole, the result of an opposition between its negative pole, the force of repulsion and terror expressed in the second section, and its positive pole, the predominant force of hope and faith expressed most clearly in the fifth; and in Section IV there is the high-pressure discharge between the poles, the poetic shock of the union of opposites: terror transformed into awe.

The dominant symbol of the poem is Fire—the Fire of Hell, the purifying Fire of Purgatory, the Fire which St. John of the Cross used as a symbol for divine love, the Fire of the Descent of the Holy Ghost at Pentecost. And—less obviously, perhaps—*Little Gidding*, as much as *The Dry Salvages*, works through its symbolism. In tone and poetic method it seems to combine the direct 'Quartet' intimacy of *East Coker*[1] and the impersonal power of *The Dry Salvages.*

The opening is perhaps the flower of a seed cast aside in the second section of *East Coker*; if so, the developed symbolism of 'midwinter spring'[2] is the very reverse of a 'periphrastic study'. That dismissed strophe spoke of a disturbing and unexpected stirring of life in the autumnal decline of age, and of the illusion of the expected 'serenity'. The superb symbolism here is of wider application. In the last

[1] Compare the *tone* of the two passages beginning:

In that open field
If you do not come too close, . . .
East Coker, I

and

If you came this way, . . .
Little Gidding, I

[2] The symbolism first occurs, I think, in *Murder in the Cathedral,* there used in a completely different context:

Spring has come in winter. Snow in the branches
Shall float as sweet as blossoms. Ice along the ditches
Mirror the sunlight. . . .
(*op. cit.* p. 24).

lines of *The Dry Salvages* we were back, symbolically, from Water to Earth; now the new symbol flames down on the dead land, suggesting a condition which is both death and birth, and so beyond death and birth. We are ordinarily aware of the passing of time in the procession of the seasons; but here there is a transitory moment of winter which seems like spring, and in this union of opposite seasons, in the suspension of time and space, we have a moment, a condition which seems timeless. It is not 'spring' in time; it is not the awakening of the life of nature. It is a spiritual awakening, an earnest of eternity: the *soul's* sap quivers:

> . . . the unimaginable
> Zero summer

(how well found and placed is that *Zero*!) is the heaven 'which flesh cannot endure'.

> For most of us, there is only the unattended
> Moment, the moment in and out of time, . . .

One such moment has been grasped and held in this first strophe. There is

> . . . no wind, but pentecostal fire
> In the dark time of the year.

In the opening strophes of *The Dry Salvages* the 'turning world' was forced upon our attention, the 'stillness' only hinted. Here not only is the 'still point' realized afresh, but we see in the intensity of the symbolism the radiant power within it, the centripetal force it generates.

After this concentrated symbolic expression, there is verse reminiscent of that haunting cadenced speech which was perfected in *East Coker*—speech as suggestive in its premonitory rhythmic insistence as the controlled tremor in the voice of a friend who is to convince us, with apprehensive precision, that he has seen a ghost. But it is something more surprising than a ghost that the poet has seen; he speaks abstractedly of our route to Little Gidding, and of the place we come from, but he is thinking of what we *are*, where we start in another sense. He thinks, too, that we have not 'put off sense and notion'; he cauterizes our materialism. As the moment of 'midwinter spring' is a significant point in time, so Little Gidding—the village of Eastern England which was, in the second quarter of the seventeenth century, the home of Nicholas Ferrar's religious community—is a significant point in space. But—as the last two lines of the section emphasize—neither space nor time is in question; nor is matter—the pig-sty, the dull façade and the tombstone. It is what the remains of the old buildings stand for that matters. The allusion to Charles the Martyr coming at night time, a broken king, to Ferrar's devout community[1] sets up the first vibration; this—more remote—the second:

And what you thought you came for
Is only a shell, a husk of meaning
From which the purpose breaks only when it is fulfilled
If at all. Either you had no purpose
Or the purpose is beyond the end you figured
And is altered in fulfilment.

Then we are on the edge of the world, looking into the darkness which shall be the light,

There are other places
Which also are the world's end, some at the sea jaws,
Or over a dark lake, in a desert or a city—
But this is the nearest, in place and time,
Now and in England. . . .

with, to intensify the vision, the amazing richness of association of the second and third lines—the drowning at sea of *The Dry Salvages*, crashing from the air, death in war in desert or city, and a hint of the darkness which was over all the earth until the ninth hour. Palestine is suggested, but not only Palestine. And perhaps I am not alone in thinking of the associations of the *desert* in *Ash-Wednesday:* spiritual thirst, and the means of its satisfaction in a condition of aridity, away from the world.

[1] Charles I visited Little Gidding, the village of Huntingdonshire, in 1646, shortly before he surrendered to the Scots army at Newark. He had been to its religious house before (in 1633), and in his desolation he remembered the peaceful hours he had spent there. 'Very privately, in the darkness of night, he came once more to Gidding' (Carter: *Life of Nicholas Ferrar*).

(I am indebted to some correspondence quoted in *Scrutiny* (Winter, 1943) for most of the information contained in this note.)

The reader who has followed the sequence so far will not be held up in the remaining lines of the section; but he may well at a first reading be puzzled by the three stanzas which follow. (He may even pause to wonder—though I hope he will not—whether there is a pun in the fourth line of the first of them.) The first thing is to get an impression of the *whole section* of which they are a part. And Mr. D. W. Harding has very clearly indicated what Eliot is driving at, in his excellent review of the poem:[1]

> 'Section II can be regarded as the *logical* starting point of the whole poem. It deals with the desolation of death and the futility of life for those who have had no conviction of spiritual values in their life's work. First come three sharply organized riming stanzas to evoke, by image and idea but without literal statement, our sense of the hopeless death of air, earth, fire and water, seen not only as the elements of man's existence but as the means of his destruction and dismissal. The tone having been set by these stanzas, there opens a narrative passage describing the dreary bitterness in which a life of literary culture can end if it has brought no sense of spiritual values. The life presented is one, such as Mr. Eliot's own, of effort after clear speech and exact thought, and the passage amounts to a shuddering "There but for the grace of God go I". . . . What the humanist's ghost sees in his life are futility, isolation and guilt on account of his self-assertive prowess—"Which once you took for exercise of virtue"—and the measure of aggression against others which that must bring. . . .'

This section reminds us how much 'every new attempt is a wholly new start', for the verse-forms in both its parts are new in Mr. Eliot's published work. In the first we notice the power of the concentrated symbolism,[2] and the dead shudder as each stanza halts at the elemental death. The lines are controlled, impersonal, bare; but they *suggest* a personal horror so intense that only the shade in the following part can state it explicitly:

[1] *Scrutiny*, Spring, 1943.

[2] The symbolism in the first and possibly in the last stanza is intensified, I feel, by air-raid memories.

> Let me disclose the gifts reserved for age
> To set a crown upon your lifetime's effort.
> First, the cold friction of expiring sense
> Without enchantment, offering no promise
> But bitter tastelessness of shadow fruit
> As body and soul begin to fall asunder.
> Second, the conscious impotence of rage
> At human folly, and the laceration
> Of laughter at what ceases to amuse. . . .

Remembering the imagery of *East Coker*, we see the first stanza as an expression of inner and outer decay: human feeling, sensuous pleasure, love, have burnt out, leaving only an old man's perishable memory. All the richness of human life in the past seems to have faded; there is only a memory of what the past felt as permanent. Man's constructions—*the wall, the wainscot and the mouse* suggest the decayed manor, once the centre of traditional village life—become dust breathed in the air. There is only a Void which, more than despair, terrifies the imagination.

This is the death of air.

The tears of sorrow and dryness of thirst are as futile as the contest of *flood and drouth.* Both man's struggles and the restlessness of the elements are fruitless, and nature itself seems to be aware of their absurdity: hollow laughter comes from the gaping earth. All is vanity.

This is the death of earth.

Agriculture, urban culture and religious tradition—all seemingly effete—are supplanted. The Eucharist, no longer regarded as an offering of the body and blood of Christ in perpetual memory of His sacrifice on the Cross, appears to be mocked in the destruction. The destroyed sanctuary becomes a symbol of desecration.

This is the death of water and fire.

The four 'elements'—air, earth, water and fire[1]—which are the means of destruction are themselves destroyed. There is nothing so positive here as a vision of the Last Day. There

[1] I think it was Mr. Henry Reed who suggested that the 'four elements' are, in that order, leading symbols of *Four Quartets.*

is only utter negation, a spiritual despair which the whole of the rest of the poem fights—which in effect is destroyed by the rest of the section.

Mr. Harding's comment on the verse of the next part also deserves quoting:

> 'The verse in this narrative passage, with its regular measure and insistent alliteration, so effective for combining the macabre with the urbane and dreary, is a way to indicate *and a way to control* the pressure of urgent misery and self-disgust.'

Its form, one is tempted to say, is a model for any future translator of Dante: an adaptation of *terza rima* to the English language—an adaptation in which assonance, anaphora and balance of phrase take the place of rhyme. The 'debt' to Dante is suggested here and there in the phrasing; and Mr. Eliot presumably had in mind the Brunetto Latini episode of the *Inferno*, Canto XV,[1] and 'those whom the wind leads' of Canto V. But it is transformation rather than imitation, and there is none of the consciously brilliant *jeu d'allusions* of *Burbank*. An allusion which is necessary for understanding, such as the allusion to the purification of purgatory in

> From wrong to wrong the exasperated spirit
> Proceeds, unless restored by that refining fire
> Where you must move in measure, like a dancer. . . .

is made sufficiently clear by the lines themselves;[2] and its effect depends on the associations which the fire symbol has elsewhere in the poem. (The adaptation of a phrase from *Hamlet* in the last line is a matter of intelligent craftsmanship which, like the borrowings of Chaucer—or, for that matter, Shakespeare—justifies itself.)

The second and third lines of this part recall

> . . . the trailing
> Consequence of further days and hours, . . .

[1] See . . . *lo cotto aspetto* (' the baked features ') and *Siete voi qui* . . .? (' Are you here . . .? ') of ll. 26 and 30.

[2] Mr. Eliot points out that he had in mind here the Arnaut Daniel episode of the *Purgatorio* (Canto XXVI), the last line of which was quoted in *The Waste Land* (l. 427). The shade of the Provençal poet circles the Mountain of Purgatory in the fire which purifies the lustful. He pauses to speak to Dante: ' Then dived he back into that fire which refines them ' (*Poi s'ascose nel foco che gli affina*).

and the conquered despair of Section II of *The Dry Salvages*. And the lines which follow relate the section to the rest of *Little Gidding* :

> After the dark dove with the flickering tongue
> Had passed below the horizon of his homing . . .

The *flickering* suggests the tongues of flame, and *dark* the mystery of the Holy Spirit, the Comforter 'whom the world cannot receive'. The soul is far from the 'world's end'—

> Between three districts whence the smoke arose.[1]

Before the end of the Dark Night there is one image to be purged: the image of the futilely striving autonomous self.

Heightened by the coolness of the verse there is a nightmare uncertainty about the identity of the apparition of the 'dead master'

> Whom I had known, forgotten, half recalled
> Both one and many; in the brown baked features
> The eyes of a familiar compound ghost
> Both intimate and unidentifiable.

'He' appears in the form of Brunetto Latini, yet is 'both one and many', uniting 'eminent men of letters' and others who have suffered or who will suffer the torments of despair he describes. And as Mr. Harding has already pointed out, the ghost in its 'intimate' aspect is the Eliot that might have been.[2] The poet echoes Dante's words, which echo back:

> So I assumed a double part, and cried
> And heard another's voice cry: 'What! are *you* here?'
> Although we were not.

This is superb phantasmagoria, and yet the language is beautifully clear. The 'double part' is the part of Dante and

[1] 'Why "*three* districts"?' asks a friend whose pertinacity in plying me with questions has been most helpful. Does he perhaps want me to answer: 'Hell, Purgatory, and between them, London'? Or should I refer him to the London districts mentioned in *Burnt Norton*, Section III? I prefer to take this part as *dream*. That *three* is to me a fine touch, suggesting in its context the allegory of Dante. The suggestiveness of the number *three* matters more, in the poetry, than the districts themselves.

[2] There is little point in making a list of 'unidentifiable' possibilities, but some may find significance in the fact that 'To purify the dialect of the tribe' is Mallarmé's *Donner un sens plus pur aux mots de la tribu* (*Le Tombeau d'Edgar Poe*).

the part of Eliot, and at the same time the answer seems an echo. The last half-line is a sudden communication to the reader that the meeting is outside time and space:

> . . . at this intersection time
> Of meeting nowhere, no before and after,
> We trod the pavement in a dead patrol.

The reader will not miss the brilliant innuendoes:

> Too strange to each other for misunderstanding,

and

> . . . as the passage now presents no hindrance
> To the spirit unappeased and peregrine
> Between two worlds become much like each other,[1]

the second one, cathartic in its effect of combined terror and consolation, a dramatically appropriate hint of *The Waste Land.*

The section leaves an overwhelming impression—less of the immediacy of its horror than of the distancing of it. We cannot complain that the 'detachment from self . . .' so serenely defined in the next section has *merely* been defined: the poet has been 'someone other'. The transition here is similar to the transition in Section II of *The Dry Salvages*, with a deeper effect of contrast. As before, reflection is based on the experience just rendered. 'Detachment' is, with lucid metaphor, distinguished from 'indifference', and in a passage which takes up the distinction between love and desire at the end of *Burnt Norton* and the thought of the last section of *East Coker*, we see that remembrance of the being of the past may free our motives of longing for personal eminence, influence, or possession; we see our own action in relation to other action and so no longer exaggerate the importance of limited ends

[1] The *two worlds* are, I take it, this world of suffering and a world of suffering beyond—whether Hell or Purgatory depends on us (see Section IV). Compare Agatha's words in *The Family Reunion:*

> You and I,
> My dear, may very likely meet again
> In our wanderings in the neutral territory
> Between two worlds.

(*op. cit.* p. 121).

or arrogantly strive after the unattainable. We free ourselves from worldly desires, achieve detachment

For a further union . . .

We free ourselves, too, from a longing to restore the past, and gain strength rather from what was potential than from what was actual in it:

See, now they vanish,
The faces and places, with the self which, as it could, loved them,
To become renewed, transfigured, in another pattern.

And a voice which seems to come both from the distant past, from Chaucer's England, and from the present, speaks of these human limitations with sonorous conviction and purity:

Sin is Behovely, but
All shall be well, and
All manner of thing shall be well.[1]

In that resonant paradox which in the first line urges the reader's concentration, Eliot is 'getting as much as possible of the whole weight of the history of the language behind his word'—and not only of the *language.* We are impelled to grasp this re-affirmation of humility and acceptance of the will of God: the people of the past were imperfect, but so are we; together—

All touched by a common genius,
United in the strife which divided them;

—they are 'Behovely' to us, they have something to give to us which we need. Even 'Sin is Behovely' if we profit by what we see is evil—by rejecting the evil. Then 'All shall be well'. It is in this sense that evils are seen as *necessary*—as a means of human discipline, just as the exposure of the evil of despair in the second section of the poem is a means of discipline. All this is implied by the statement, and I suppose it has been

[1] The last line comes from *The Shewings* of Lady Julian of Norwich, a late fourteenth-century recluse.

said many times before in other words; but I have never seen it more memorably expressed than in those three lines.

The poet thinks 'again' of Little Gidding and of the seventeenth-century figures which come to his mind—the 'broken' Charles visiting the community, his supporters on the scaffold, perhaps the blind author of *Paradise Lost*—but they are not named: the remoteness of the reference suggests that they are

> . . . renewed, transfigured, in another pattern.

So, we remember,

> This is the use of memory:
> For liberation—— . . .

and there is no escape into the past:

> Why should we celebrate
> These dead men more than the dying?

Nor is there any desire to restore an old order. What we can take from 'these dead men'—failures though they may have been in the eyes of the world—is a spiritual example completed beyond this life.

And upon this cool meditation the Dove descends bringing Fire. The protagonist faces, instead of the impotence of despair of Section II, the overwhelming positive force of divine love, a terrifying spiritual power beyond humanity to which humanity must surrender, or be consumed in the inferno:

> Who then devised the torment? Love.
> Love is the unfamiliar Name
> Behind the hands that wove
> The intolerable shirt of flame
> Which human power cannot remove.
> We only live, only suspire
> Consumed by either fire or fire.

The alternatives are the fire of purification and the fire of damnation. The imagery of the fine middle lines of the stanza[1] develops the message of *East Coker*:

[1] The superb metaphor of the fourth and fifth lines may be associated with the death of Hercules. The shirt of Nessus, the centaur promised, would always

. . . if we do well, we shall
Die of the absolute paternal care . . .

Of the last section the first sentence is general, the second minutely particular, and both co-operate to express the one vision. All that we think of as happening in time is seen to form a pattern so complete that you cannot say where any part of it starts or finishes: you can only infer that the beginning and end of the whole pattern is purpose. The strophe is both a development of the statement of *East Coker*,

In my end is my beginning

and a re-creation of the phrase 'world without end'. Human life is part of the pattern, not a sequence in time determined by physical dissolution. There is therefore no fear of death *in itself*, and imagining

Every poem an epitaph . . .

is, like the related line in *The Dry Salvages*

(And the time of death is every moment)

the reverse of 'depressing'. Why should we be frightened of death as children are frightened by the dark? It is 'where we start'; it is a movement 'into another intensity'. And that movement is always taking place *now*:

. . . And any action
Is a step to the block, to the fire, down the sea's throat
Or to an illegible stone: and that is where we start.
We die with the dying:
See, they depart, and we go with them.
We are born with the dead:
See, they return, and bring us with them.

Thus—as in the masterly parenthesis on the 'sentence that is right'—is the emphasis thrown on present action. But the

---

preserve Hercules' love: it preserved his love by tormenting him to death. He built his own funeral pyre; the shirt of blood became a shirt of flame; and he was taken up to Olympus.

essence of what is consolidated—and with the weight of the whole sequence behind it—is outside time:

> The moment of the rose and the moment of the yew-tree
> Are of equal duration. A people without history
> Is not redeemed from time, for history is a pattern
> Of timeless moments. So, while the light fails
> On a winter's afternoon, in a secluded chapel
> History is now and England.

The first sentence resolves the contrast between the associations and span of life of the rose and the yew-tree in that fruitful union of the two images; and if we remember what has gone before, the depth of its suggestiveness cannot be measured. I can only indicate its meaning. As the thousand years of the yew-tree are equivalent in value to the hour of the rose's perfection, so it is not duration that matters: it is that quality and intensity of life which, if it exists in a moment, exists in every moment. Thus the poetry realizes the conception of the *timeless*. And if we had no inheritance from the past of the kind that was contemplated in Section III, we should lack the redeeming benefit of those moments of inspiration which mark the greatness of a people, moments in which history triumphs over time.

With the line that is left to echo after this passage[1] we are beyond the chapel of Little Gidding, beyond England, beyond history. From the vantage point of the last strophe we can survey the whole sequence. The poet unites themes and images from all that has gone before in order to express the 'condition of complete simplicity': after a reminder of *East Coker*, we are back at the beginning, at the vision in *Burnt Norton* of the Earthly Paradise. And in the last lines there is the hope of union with God. In that union, divine love and human love meet: 'the fire and the rose are one'.

> We shall not cease from exploration
> And the end of all our exploring
> Will be to arrive where we started

[1] The line is quoted from *The Cloud of Unknowing*, the work of an anonymous mystic of fourteenth-century England who translated the *Mystical Theology* of Dionysius.

And know the place for the first time.
Through the unknown, remembered gate
When the last of earth left to discover
Is that which was the beginning;
At the source of the longest river
The voice of the hidden waterfall
And the children in the apple-tree
Not known, because not looked for
But heard, half-heard, in the stillness
Between two waves of the sea.
Quick now, here, now, always—
A condition of complete simplicity
(Costing not less than everything)
And all shall be well and
All manner of thing shall be well
When the tongues of flame are in-folded
Into the crowned knot of fire
And the fire and the rose are one.[1]

And so the sequence ends, with lines that approach what Mr. Eliot has called 'the highest point that poetry has ever reached or ever can reach'—the conclusion of the *Paradiso*. And even an approach to that point is a triumph. The joy felt in these lines has been won, the faith has come of facing despair and conquering it. And it is one measure of the permanence of *Four Quartets* that the despair which has been faced and conquered is not the despair of an age: 'wait without hope . . .' (the meditation of *East Coker*) not only directs us to bear to-day's darkness patiently, but shows us a stage of a man's spiritual progress in *any* age. There is no easy faith in these poems. If faith is 'the substance of things hoped for', then you have it in these last lines: the substance.

[1] . . . *the children in the apple-tree:* it is of little importance here that the poet appears to be drawing on an early minor poem (*Landscapes, I*: *Collected Poems, 1909–1935*, p. 148). The line takes us back to the vision of *Burnt Norton*, I; and its point is that it takes us *further back* than ' the bitter apple and the bite in the apple ' of *The Dry Salvages*. And I think that Eliot follows St. John of the Cross in associating the *apple-tree* at once with the Tree of Paradise and with the Tree of the Cross: in spite of the Fall, the Redemption makes possible the ' complete simplicity ' or wholeness ' costing not less than everything '.

The *tongues of flame* of the Holy Spirit are, when they have fulfilled their purpose, *in-folded* into their Source. The three strands of the *crowned knot* symbolize the Trinity.

This brief record of several readings of *Four Quartets* has been a kind of first rehearsal—at best, an experiment in interpretation. Say we know the notes, there are many ways of playing them; and no way is perfect. No reading of poems so inexhaustible is perfect either: and what is needed to correct the deficiencies of one's personal reading is not an exchange of critical gun-fire, but quiet co-operative discussion of detail. Such co-operative reading requires patience, and a willingness to submit to a discipline of trial-and-error in the effort to reach the purest contemplation of what the poetry offers for contemplation. Eliot has squeezed out of experience and meditation a concentrate which appears in one light as philosophical or theological thought; but it is thought which is inseparable from keenness of perception and feeling, thought which hardly for one instant leaves perception and feeling behind. If it is beyond poetry, it is also beyond philosophy, for pure speculation may not touch the real springs of our being and action—depths of which most of the time we are unconscious. The motives of action and the emotions and meditations even of those of us who profess a faith are often an incoherent jumble. If these poems bring *consciousness*, if they bring awareness of what is involved in directing our lives—our contemplation and action—towards *one end*, and awareness of what such an end must be like: that, if you like, you may call the 'philosophy' —or teleology, ethics, metaphysics reconstituted. But the direct shock of the sudden vision, the delicacy and poise and compelling precision of the language, the realization of present and historic and primitive experience, of the experience of the saint and the experience of the sinner—all directed to the one end: that is what we call the poetry, and that is what makes for the consciousness. You cannot isolate the 'poetry' any more than you can isolate the 'philosophy'.

The more closely we look at the detail, the more we see *Four Quartets* as a whole in this way. Much of this book has been annotation; and annotation may be helpful at what one might call the second stage of reading. The third stage of reading is reached when we realize that 'notes' do not matter, and that the poems elucidate themselves once we begin to grasp the relation between their parts. Finally, to understand *Four Quartets* we need to live with them, and even to live by them.